Famous Leaders: Zeroes or Heroes?

capstone
classroom

BTR Zone (Bridge to Reading) is published by Capstone Classroom, 1710 Roe Crest Drive, North Mankato, Minnesota 56003 www.capstoneclassroom.com

ISBN 978-1-62521-088-3

Editorial Credits

Gene Bentdahl, designer; Eric Gohl, media researcher

Photo Credits

BigStockPhoto.com: Bill Perry, 58 (top); Corbis: Swim Ink, 17; CriaImages.com: Jay Robert Nash Collection, 46 (bottom), 51; Getty Images: DeAgostini, 13; iStockphotos: Duncan Walker, 23, pictore, cover (bottom left), 38, Ralf Hettler, 45, 59 (top), Steven Wynn, 22; Library of Congress: cover (top left, top right, bottom right), 26, 46 (top), 48, 56, 57, 59 (middle & bottom); Newscom: akg-images, 9, 29, 40, CNP/Arnie Sachs, 55, George Munday/Design Pics, 36, Oronoz/Album, 20, Prisma/Album, 32-33, Rabatti-Domingie/akg-images, cover (top middle), 14, World History Archive, 6, ZUMA Press/Donatella Giagnori, 18; Shutterstock: Georgios Kollidas, 30, Login, 4, lynea, 10, Vladimir Korostyshevskiy, 58 (bottom), Vladimir Wrangel, 8; Wikipedia: Hermitage Museum, 25, NARA, 52, Public Domain, cover (bottom middle), 34, 42

Design Elements: Shutterstock

About the Cover

top left to right: Winston Churchill, Cleopatra, Joan of Arc
bottom left to right: Maximilien Robespierre, Napoleon Bonaparte, Richard Nixon

Printed in the United States of America in North Mankato, Minnesota.
032013   007223CGF13

TABLE OF CONTENTS

Introduction

For better or worse, powerful leaders have changed our world. Sometimes they have great plans to seek out what is best for their people. Other times, they try to gain complete power while ignoring citizens' **rights** to speak or act freely.

Should we judge these leaders on the basis of their achievements? Or should we consider their character as well? Were these people heroes or villains? What makes a great leader? Read their stories and decide for yourself.

right · something the law allows people to do, such as the right to vote or the right to speak freely

ancient drawing of Amenhotep IV and Nefertiti

How Long Ago Was That?

The initials BC following a leader's birth or death dates stand for "before Christ." It means that date comes before the birth of Jesus. Figuring out how long ago a BC date was is simple. Just add the date to the current year, then add one more. So Nefertiti died in 1330 BC. 2014 + 1330 + 1 = 3,345 years ago

Nefertiti
(about 1370 BC–1330 BC)

King Amenhotep III ruled the country of Egypt for almost 40 years. When he died, his oldest son, Amenhotep IV, became king. Amenhotep needed a wife. He looked for a strong girl from a noble family. He found Nefertiti (nef-ri-TEE-tee), whose name means "the beautiful woman has come."

For hundreds of years, the ancient Egyptians worshipped many gods. About four years after Nefertiti became queen, her husband changed his religious beliefs. He came to believe that Aten, the sun god, was the most important god.

A New Home

Amenhotep decided to leave the religious capital of Thebes and build a new city to honor Aten. He also changed his name to Akhenaten to honor the god. The royal couple designed the new city. Chariots carried the royal family to their new palace. As many as 50,000 Egyptians moved to this new city to serve the king and queen.

Nefertiti was a strong leader. She drove her own chariot. She was honored with statues as big as her husband's. In some pictures she was even shown killing Egypt's enemies.

ancient sculpture of Nefertiti

Leading Fact!

Most girls in ancient Egypt married young. Historians believe Nefertiti was about 15 years old when she became queen. Amenhotep IV was about the same age.

Nefertiti is shown as a strong, independent woman in many drawings and paintings.

Nefertiti Disappears

For the first 12 years of her married life, Nefertiti was shown as happy with her husband and six daughters. They had plenty of food, many palaces, and the riches of Egypt.

Sometime after this Nefertiti disappeared from record. Around the same time, artists carved pictures of King Akhenaten with a new king, Smenkhkare. Some historians argue that Nefertiti was in fact the new king. They believe she changed her name and became co-ruler of ancient Egypt.

Julius Caesar

Julius Caesar
(100 BC–44 BC)

Julius Caesar is one of the most famous leaders in history. He marched throughout the continents of Europe and Asia, defeating his enemies and claiming territory. Under Caesar's rule the nation known as the Roman **Empire** grew. The empire controlled much of southern Europe and northern sections of the continent of Africa.

The Power of Rome

Caesar made Rome the most powerful empire on Earth. In 46 BC he was elected to be the absolute ruler, known as a **dictator**, for 10 years.

As Rome's dictator Caesar developed a new system of law. He built roads and libraries and developed the calendar that is used today. Caesar enjoyed power and personal glory.

empire · a large territory ruled by a powerful leader

dictator · someone who has complete control of a country, often ruling it unjustly

Too Powerful?

Caesar's thirst for power led people to fear him. He showed no mercy to the people he **conquered**. He turned millions of people into Roman **slaves**. As dictator, Caesar gave orders that he expected others to follow and obey without question.

Even Rome's rich landowners feared Caesar. They worried that he would take away their wealth and power. A group of leaders called senators thought Caesar had become too powerful. On March 15, 44 BC, they stabbed Caesar to death.

conquer · to defeat and take control of an enemy

slave · a person owned by another person

Caesar was killed by senators who feared the leader's power was too great.

Servants traveled with Cleopatra wherever she went.

Cleopatra
(69 BC–30 BC)

Cleopatra VII was the last queen of Egypt in ancient times. She ruled from 51 BC to 30 BC. As queen, Cleopatra was charming and smart. She also wanted to keep her power at any cost.

Cleopatra's father, Ptolemy XII, was the king, or **pharaoh**, of Egypt. When her father died, she and her younger brother, Ptolemy XIII, ruled Egypt. In 48 BC, Ptolemy XIII was killed, and Cleopatra controlled Egypt.

Cleopatra traveled to the city of Rome in 41 BC. She knew the Roman nation, called the Roman Empire, could be a powerful friend to Egypt. To show off her riches and power, she dressed like a goddess and rode in a golden ship.

pharaoh · a king in ancient Egypt

A Life of Luxury

Cleopatra and Roman ruler Marc Antony fell in love. As rulers they had many comforts and **luxuries**. They hosted feasts and parties. They had jewels, gold, and other riches.

Battle for Power

A Roman leader named Octavian wanted Antony's power. He said Cleopatra wanted to take over Rome. Octavian declared war on Egypt. In 31 BC, ships from Rome and Egypt met in a great sea battle. By 30 BC, Octavian had captured Egypt.

Cleopatra ruled Egypt for 21 years. She gained riches and fame. But she lost control of Egypt to the Roman Empire.

luxury · something that is not needed but adds great comfort

Cleopatra and Antony's relationship is often called the greatest love story of all time.

Nero

Nero
(37–68)

As a young Roman ruler, or **emperor**, Nero started out well. The 17-year-old leader lowered how much money people paid to the government. He also made the killing of criminals illegal. He gave government leaders called senators more power. He even gave money to cities in need. But he quickly became the most hated emperor of all.

Unstoppable

Nero would do anything for wealth and power. He took land for himself and ordered the landowners killed. Nero killed anyone who seemed to threaten his power. He ordered the deaths of his mother, stepbrother, and one of his wives. Sometimes he put on a costume or disguise and walked the streets of Rome. He would then stab random people.

emperor · a male ruler of a country or group of countries

The fire of Rome destroyed much of the city. Nero later built a huge palace in the center of the burned area.

A City on Fire

In the year 64, a fire swept through Rome. Many Romans suspected that Nero set it so he could rebuild the city the way he wanted. Nero falsely blamed **Christians**, people who follow the teachings of Jesus, for the blaze. He tortured and killed many Christians.

After the fire Nero's enemies planned to kill him. Nero learned of the plan. He killed many of those plotting against him. But soon the army turned against Nero. He knew he could not survive as emperor. Nero killed himself before his enemies could kill him.

Christian · a person who follows a religion based on the teachings of Jesus

Young Joan of Arc led a French army against the English during the Hundred Years' War.

Joan of Arc
(about 1412–1431)

Joan of Arc was a deeply religious 13-year-old French girl. In the early 1400s, she claimed to see bright **visions** and hear voices that told her she must save France.

Winning the French Crown

Charles VII was next in line to be crowned king of France. But the English king, Henry VI, also wanted the crown. At age 17 Joan told Charles about her plan to save France. Although Joan was poor and uneducated, Charles listened to her plan to help him become king. Charles gave Joan an army to attack France's English enemies. England was defeated and soon Charles VII became king of France.

Joan convinced King Charles that God spoke to her.

At that time women were expected to be mothers, but Joan led soldiers into battle. Joan's unselfish goals, faith, and love of France persuaded many others to follow her lead.

vision · something seen, as in a dream

One year after Charles VII became king, Joan was captured and jailed by English soldiers. She was turned over to France for trial. A French **priest** who supported the British sentenced Joan of Arc to death by fire.

Deserted!

The French did not speak out on Joan's behalf. Her army deserted her. Even Charles VII was silent. At first church leaders had praised Joan's religious faith. But then they became angry that Joan wore men's clothes and claimed that God spoke directly to her. They did not help her. In 1431 Joan of Arc was burned to death for being a witch. She was only 19 years old.

Leading Fact!

In 1920 the Roman Catholic Church made Joan of Arc a **saint**.

priest · a member of a church who leads church services and performs religious rites

saint · a person honored by the Catholic church for his or her holiness

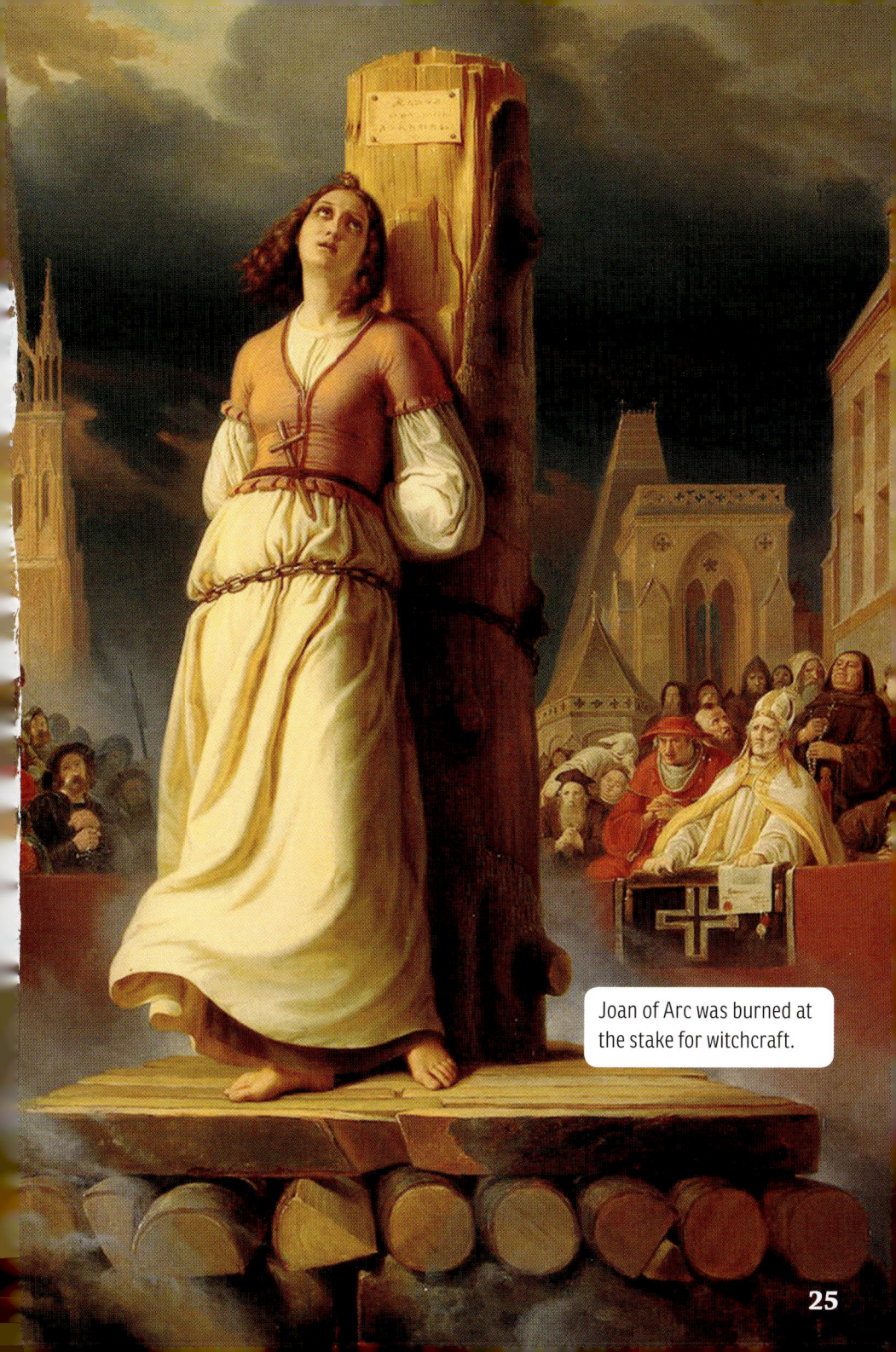

Joan of Arc was burned at the stake for witchcraft.

Isabella (center) met with Columbus (left) and listened to his plans to discover a new route to Asia.

Queen Isabella
(1451–1504)

As a child in the 1400s, Princess Isabella of the Spanish country of Castile heard stories about Joan of Arc. Like Joan, Isabella grew up to be a deeply religious woman with strong ideas.

Equal Power

Isabella refused to marry the man her father had chosen for her. Instead, she chose Ferdinand of the Spanish country of Aragon. After they were married, Isabella and Ferdinand united their two countries into one strong Spanish nation. They ruled as equal partners. Isabella's courage, intelligence, and beauty impressed the Spanish people.

Isabella brought wealth, law, and order to Spain. She also supported exploration. Under her rule Christopher Columbus sailed to the New World, an area that is now known as the Americas. Gradually, Spain became a world power.

Leading Fact!

It took Columbus more than six years to convince Queen Isabella and her advisors to give him the money to explore the New World.

Isabella wanted to spread Christianity throughout the New World. She sent priests to the Americas with explorers. Their mission was to make the native people there Christians.

The Inquisition

In Spain Isabella appointed Tomás de Torquemada as the chief investigator of the Spanish **Inquisition**. His job was to check people's religious beliefs. Anyone who was not Catholic was forced to either become Catholic or leave Spain. Those who refused both options were tortured and killed.

Isabella changed Spain forever. Some of the changes did great good while others caused long-lasting harm. Some people say Isabella was right to impose her beliefs, but others say she was cruel and evil. What do you think?

Leading Fact!

During the Spanish Inquisition, between 160,000 and 180,000 Jewish people were driven out of Spain because they were not Christian.

Under Isabella's orders Tomás de Torquemada (right) forced many Jews out of Spain.

Inquisition · a former court of the Catholic Church that often accused and cruelly punished people for not following the church from the late 1400s to the early 1800s

Hernán Cortés

Hernán Cortés
(1485–1547)

Hernán Cortés (er-NAHN kawr-TEZ) was an explorer and a **conquistador**. Conquistadors were Spanish leaders who took over areas in the Americas. Cortés wanted to conquer the Aztec Empire, a thriving nation located in what is now Mexico.

Finding Tenochtitlán

On November 8, 1519, Cortés and his men looked down onto a valley. A great city sat on an island in a large lake. White stone buildings seemed to rise out of the water.

Cortés and his men had traveled more than 275 miles (443 kilometers) into what is now the country of Mexico. They had marched over high mountains and through thick forests. Their journey was over. They were looking down at Tenochtitlán, the capital city of the Aztecs.

Many of the men were worried. They did not know how their small group could conquer the great city. But Cortés would not give up. He was ready to take over the Aztec Empire and claim the land for the country of Spain.

conquistador · a military leader in the Spanish conquest of North and South America during the 1500s

The Conquest

The Aztec leader, or emperor, welcomed Cortés. But soon Cortés took the emperor prisoner. On December 26, 1520, Cortés led his men to Tenochtitlán. They built small boats and took over the lake around the city. With no one able to get in or out, many Aztecs ran out of food. Others died from smallpox or other diseases.

Cortés soon realized that he had to destroy Tenochtitlán to get rid of the Aztecs' hiding places. Cortés' men burned all of the buildings. The beautiful city was reduced to ashes. Thousands of people died. On August 13, 1521, Cortés conquered the Aztec Empire.

Cortés (front left) captured the Aztec leader Montezuma.

Marie Antoinette

peasant · a poor person who worked on or owned a small farm

Marie Antoinette
(1755–1793)

In April 1774 King Louis XV died. Suddenly, Louis Auguste and Marie Antoinette were the new king and queen of France. He was 19, and she was just 18.

Life as a Queen

Marie had 500 servants waiting on her. Her servants woke her up, dressed her, and fixed her hair. The queen did not like all the attention, but she loved choosing new clothes and jewelry.

The queen and king lived nearly all of their lives in palaces near the city of Versailles. They had everything they wanted. They never saw how the French people lived in the countryside.

Cutting Back

During Marie's years at Versailles, France went through several droughts and a very cold winter. The poor farmers, known as **peasants**, were desperate for food. People were angry at how much money the king and queen were spending. Marie let go 173 servants and ordered fewer dresses. Still, people believed she was spending too much on clothing, fine furniture, and jewelry.

In October 1789 about 6,000 women marched from the city of Paris to the palace at Versailles. They demanded bread for their families. The mob attacked the palace guards and insisted Marie and Louis go to Paris.

Once in Paris, Marie, Louis, and their two children became prisoners of the new government that had formed. They were held in a castle called Les Tuileries. Many people argued that they should be killed.

Marie Antoinette (back right), Louis (center) and their children were held as prisoners.

A Daring Escape

In the early morning hours of June 21, 1791, Marie and her family disguised themselves and fled Paris. They headed to the country of Austria, where Marie was born. In the town of Varennes, townspeople recognized the family and took them prisoner. The unsuccessful escape made the French people even angrier with the king and queen.

Found Guilty

The family spent the next two years under constant guard. In December 1792, the new government sentenced Louis to death. On October 16, 1793, Marie was found guilty of betraying her country, an act called **treason**. Later that day, she was put to death.

Many experts believe Marie was not to blame for the country's money problems. However, she became an easy target for the peasants' anger.

treason · the crime of betraying your country

Maximilien Robespierre

rebel · to fight against the established government

Maximilien Robespierre
(1758–1794)

New leaders were needed after the French people **rebelled** against the government and forced King Louis Auguste and Queen Marie Antoinette from power. By 1793, Maximilien Robespierre (mak-seem-mee-LYAN ROHBZ-peer) was one of the most powerful new leaders.

"Reign of Terror"

At first Robespierre believed a peaceful change in French government was possible. But the people leading the change, also known as rebels, had many enemies inside and outside of the country of France. Robespierre decided that arresting and killing these enemies was the only way to keep power. He helped start a time of killing, known as the "Reign of Terror," across the country.

From Bad to Worse

People who seemed to threaten the rule of the rebel forces were arrested. Many were killed. The killings started with France's former royalty. As the terror spread, priests, merchants, and peasants were also arrested.

Robespierre (in the cart) was arrested for his actions and sentenced to death.

Guilty!

In 1794 Robespierre took the Reign of Terror further. He supported a law allowing the government to execute, or kill, people without proving they had done something wrong. Thousands of people were put to death.

As executions grew more frequent, citizens panicked. It seemed the slightest mistake could cost someone his or her life. People were starting to think that Robespierre had gone too far. Though quite powerful, he was no longer a popular leader.

A Deadly List

In his last speech, Robespierre claimed to have a list of traitors, or people who had gone against him. But he refused to hand over the list. Afraid their names were on the list, other leaders arrested Robespierre. They sentenced him to death, as he had done to so many people before him.

Napoleon Bonaparte

Napoleon Bonaparte
(1769–1821)

Napoleon Bonaparte (nuh-POH-lee-uhn BON-uh-part) was just a teenager when he joined the French army, but he quickly rose to power.

Making Good Laws

By 1795 Napoleon was a leader known as a general. He led soldiers to the country of Italy, where they defeated the army from the country of Austria. Then he headed to the country of Egypt with 35,000 men. After defeating the enemy there, Napoleon returned to the country of France to take control of the government there.

Napoleon's government was based on his ideas of fairness. Napoleon set up a new tax system. A tax system is how a government collects money from its people to pay for public services, such as schools and police. He allowed people to believe in any religion. He brought back law and order through a strong police force. Napoleon's system of law, known as the **Napoleonic Code**, spread throughout the continent of Europe.

Napoleonic Code · a system of law created by Napoleon Bonaparte

Napoleon achieved victory in Egypt in 1798. But his success did not last long. In 1801 the army from the country of Great Britain drove Napoleon's army out of Egypt.

Then more things began to go wrong. In June 1812 Napoleon led 611,000 troops into the country of Russia. The French troops did not have the supplies needed to survive the cold conditions. By October only 40,000 soldiers were still alive. The survivors walked home through the snow.

Surrender

Napoleon's enemies—the countries of Spain, Portugal, Great Britain, and Russia—joined together to defeat France. The countries of Sweden and Austria joined in too. By 1814 France was broke, and its armies were devastated. Napoleon surrendered and left France.

Napoleon tried to regain power at the Battle of Waterloo in 1815, but he lost there too. He surrendered to Great Britain on July 15. Napoleon died in prison, on the tiny island of Saint Helena, six years later.

Napoleon (on horseback) suffered a great
defeat in the Battle of Waterloo in Belgium.

Leading Fact!

Throughout the years people have said that
Napoleon was short. He was actually about
5 feet, 7 inches (170 centimeters) tall—slightly
taller than average for his time.

Andrew Jackson

The Indian Removal Act

Jackson signed the Indian Removal Act, which forced thousands of Indians to leave their homes. The act destroyed the Indian's way of life. Almost 17,000 Cherokee, Choctaw, Creek, and Chickasaw American Indians made the trip to Indian Territory. More than 4,000 died of disease and hunger along the way. The more than 800-mile (1,287-km) march westward is called the Trail of Tears.

Andrew Jackson
(1767–1845)

President Andrew Jackson believed that a government should represent all its people, not just the wealthy. He believed all U.S. citizens should have access to the White House and the president. No guards blocked the White House doors. No rules kept strangers from coming up to shake his hand.

Indian Removal Act

Jackson believed that the government had a responsibility to American Indians. However, he also believed that native tribes had little hope of keeping their lands. Many Americans wanted the Indian Removal Act passed. This law required American Indians to leave their homelands in the East. They would be forced to settle on land in Indian Territory in present-day Oklahoma. In 1830 President Jackson gave the American people what they wanted.

Today many historians view the Indian Removal Act as a shameful part of American history. Many tribes refused to leave their homelands. But soldiers forced them to move westward on trains, boats, and by foot.

Winston Churchill

journalist · someone who writes articles for newspapers, magazines, or TV

Parliament · a group of people who make laws and run the government in some countries

prime minister · in many nations, the head of government

treaty · an official agreement between two or more groups or countries

Winston Churchill
(1874–1965)

Winston Churchill served the country of Great Britain as a soldier and **journalist**. He was also a member of the British **Parliament**. This group of leaders made the country's laws.

War!

During World War II (1939–1945), Churchill was **prime minister**, the leader of Great Britain's government. He provided military and political leadership. He supervised the war efforts in the country and was in charge of British military operations overseas. He traveled around the world to talk with world leaders. His encouraging speeches inspired people everywhere. At the end of the war, he helped develop a **treaty**, or agreement, to keep the peace.

However during a career in the British government that lasted for more than 60 years, Churchill made mistakes.

In His Words!

In 1940 Churchill declared, "… we shall defend our Island [Great Britain], whatever the cost may be, we shall fight on the beaches … and in the streets, we shall fight in the hills; we shall never surrender …"

Too Sure of Himself?

Earlier in his career, during World War I (1914–1918), Churchill planned a military attack in the country of Turkey in 1915. More than 250,000 British, French, New Zealand, and Australian soldiers died in the failed attack. Many people claimed that Churchill had been too sure of himself and risked too much.

Many experts believe that Churchill's greatest weakness was his self-confidence. He wanted to be at the center of things and be in charge. But even when others doubted him, Churchill remained confident about his decisions.

Leading Fact!

Churchill learned to fly an airplane, but he crashed it twice in one day.

British soldiers followed Churchill's orders during the Battle of Gallipoli in Turkey. Churchill's plan was a failure, and many soldiers died.

Richard Nixon

Richard Nixon
(1913–1994)

Richard Nixon was U.S. president from 1969 to 1974. In the late 1960s, people feared the possibility of **nuclear war**. In a nuclear war, countries would use bombs that create a powerful explosion by splitting tiny **atoms**. Such a war could mean the end of the world.

Treaties and Trade

Nixon met with Leonid Brezhnev, leader of the country of the **Soviet Union**, to reduce the possibility of nuclear war. They helped create treaties that calmed people's fears.

Nixon also visited the country of China. There was no business or trade between China and the United States before Nixon's visit. Afterward, relationships improved. Many believe that Nixon's actions in 1972 created the trade program that now exists between the United States and China.

nuclear war · a fight that uses bombs that create a powerful explosion by splitting atoms

atom · a tiny particle; atoms combine together to form all things on Earth

Soviet Union · a former federation of 15 republics in eastern Europe and northern Asia

However, around 2:30 a.m. on June 17, 1972, five men broke into the Watergate Building in Washington, D.C. They installed hidden cameras in the headquarters of the **Democratic Party**, one of the country's main political parties. When the men were arrested, they said they worked for President Nixon's re-election committee. Nixon was a member of the **Republican Party**. Were they planning to spy on Nixon's opponents, the Democrats?

Did He Know?

Nixon said he knew nothing about the break-in, but the American people did not believe him. Nixon had been accused of such tricks before.

Americans were ashamed of Nixon. They no longer wanted him as their president. On August 9, 1974, Richard Nixon became the only U.S. president ever to **resign** from office.

Nixon thought he could break some laws because he was the president. Should leaders have to obey the same laws as everyone else? Should leaders be forgiven if they make mistakes?

On August 9, 1974, Nixon spoke to his staff,
telling them he was leaving office.

Democratic Party · one of the two major
political parties in the United States

Republican Party · one of the two major
political parties in the United States

resign · to give up an office or position

Some art shows Joan of Arc as a saint. Other paintings show her as a witch. Which viewpoint do you think is correct?

You Decide

What do you think of the leaders in this book? You decide if they are heroes or zeroes.

Consider This:

Joan of Arc claimed that she never personally killed anyone. However, as the leader of an army of soldiers, is she responsible for the deaths they caused?

When Winston Churchill died at age 90, a reporter noted, "He [Churchill] was never afraid to lead, and he knew that a leader must sometimes risk failure and disapproval." Are there times when a leader should take action, whether or not people approve? Are there times when a leader should have the people's approval before acting?

Was Churchill a hero or a zero?

What qualities does a good leader have?

If a world leader came to you looking for advice, what would you say?

Which world leader do you most admire and why?

Timeline of Leaders

1353–1336 BC—Nefertiti serves as queen of ancient Egypt.

50–30 BC—Cleopatra rules as the last queen of ancient Egypt.

45–44 BC—Julius Caesar leads the Roman Empire as dictator.

AD 54–68—Nero serves as emperor of the Roman Empire.

1429–1430—Joan of Arc leads the French army in victory over the English.

1474–1504—Queen Isabella rules as queen of Spain.

1518–1524—Hernán Cortés destroys the Aztec Empire and claims the area for Spain.

1773–1793—Marie Antoinette rules as queen of France.

1793–1794—Maximilien Robespierre leads a Reign of Terror through France.

1800–1814—Napoleon Bonaparte leads France as dictator.

1828–1837—Andrew Jackson serves as U.S. president.

1940–1945—Winston Churchill heads Great Britain's government as prime minister during World War II.

1969–1974—Richard Nixon serves as U.S. president.

Read More

Gaines, Ann Graham. *Richard M. Nixon: Our Thirty-Seventh President.* Presidents of the U.S.A. Mankato, Minn.: Child's World, 2009.

Pack, Mary Fisk. *Cleopatra: "Serpent of the Nile."* Thinking Girl's Treasury of Dastardly Dames. Foster City, Ca.: Goosebottom Books, 2011.

Yomtov, Nel. *Andrew Jackson: Heroic Leader or Cold-Hearted Ruler?* Perspectives on History. North Mankato, Minn.: Capstone Press, 2014.

Internet Sites

FactHound offers a safe, fun way to find Internet sites related to this book. All of the sites on FactHound have been researched by our staff.

Here's all you do:
Visit *www.facthound.com*
Type in this code: 9781625210883

Check out projects, games and lots more at
www.capstonekids.com

Glossary of Text Features

Text Feature	How to Use it
Caption: A word or group of words shown with a picture or illustration	Read a caption to understand information that may not be in the text.
Diagram: A drawing that shows or explains something	Examine a diagram to understand steps in a process, how something is made, or the parts of something.
Glossary: List of key terms with their meanings	Look up key terms in the glossary to find their meanings and to get a better understanding of the topic of the text.
Index: Alphabetical list of key terms, names, and topics in a text with their page numbers	Use the index to find pages that contain information you are looking for.
Map: A drawing that represents a place, such as a country or city	Use a map to understand relative locations and determine where events took place.
Photograph or Illustration: Visuals that are created by cameras or drawn	Examine photographs and illustrations to better understand ideas in the text that might be unclear
Subhead: Word or group of words that divides the text into sections and tells the main idea of a section	Use subheads to locate information in the text and understand how a text is organized.
Table: Represents data in a small space	Examine a table to understand data or to compare information in the text.
Table of Contents: List of the major parts of the book and their page numbers	Use a table of contents to locate general information in the text and see how the topics are organized.
Text Box: A box in the text that provides extra information about a topic	Read a text box to understand interesting or important information.
Text Style: Bold, color, or italic words in the text	Pay attention to bold, italic, and color to figure out which words in the text are important words.
Timeline: Shows events in the order in which they occurred	Use a timeline to understand the order in which events occurred or how one event led to another.

Glossary

atom (AT-uhm) • a tiny particle; atoms combine together to form all things on Earth

Christian (KRIS-chuhn) • a person who follows a religion based on the teachings of Jesus

conquer (KAHNG-kohr) • to defeat and take control of an enemy

conquistador (kon-KEYS-tuh-dor) • a military leader in the Spanish conquest of North and South America during the 1500s

Democratic Party (de-muh-KRA-tik PAR-tee) • one of two major political parties in the United States

dictator (DIK-tay-tuhr) • someone who has complete control of a country, often ruling it unjustly

emperor (EM-puhr-uhr) • a male ruler of a country or group of countries

empire (EM-pire) • a large territory ruled by a powerful leader

Inquisition (in-kwa-ZI-shun) • a former court of the Catholic Church that often accused and cruelly punished people for not following the church from the late 1400s to the early 1800s

journalist (JUR-nuhl-ist) • someone who writes articles for newspapers, magazines, or TV

luxury (LUHK-shuh-ree) • something that is not needed but adds great ease and comfort

Napoleonic Code (nah-PO-lee-on-ik KODE) • a system of law created by Napoleon Bonaparte; many countries base their laws on the Napoleonic Code

nuclear war (NOO-klee-ur WOR) • a fight that uses bombs that create a powerful explosion by splitting atoms

Parliament (PAR-luh-muhnt) • a group of people who make laws and run the government in some countries

peasant (PEZ-uhnt) • a poor person who worked on or owned a small farm

pharaoh (FAIR-oh) • a king in ancient Egypt

priest (PREEST) • a member of a church who leads church services and performs religious rites

prime minister (PRIME MIN-uh-stur) • in many nations, the head of government

rebel (ri-BEL) • to fight against the established government; a person who fights against the government is called a rebel (REB-uhl)

Republican Party (ri-PUHB-li-kuhn PAR-tee) • one of two major political parties in the United States

resign (re-ZINE) • to give up an office or position

right (RITE) • something the law allows people to do, such as the right to vote or the right to speak freely; the government cannot take away our rights

saint (SAYNT) • a person honored by the Catholic church for his or her holiness

senator (SEN-ah-tur) • a leader who helps to make the laws of a government

slave (SLAYV) • a person owned by another person; slaves were not free to choose their homes or jobs.

Soviet Union (SOH-vee-et YOON-yuhn) • a former federation of 15 republics that included Russia, Ukraine, and other nations of eastern Europe and northern Asia; also called the Union of Soviet Socialist Republics (USSR)

treason (TREE-zuhn) • the crime of betraying your country

treaty (TREE-tee) • an official agreement between two or more groups or countries

vision (VIZH-uhn) • something seen, as in a dream

Index